Anatomy of a DHS

MW01119298

A Trampling of 1st and 4th Amendment Rights

By

Garrett Kelley

Theis Education Trust, Publisher

In association with Amazon.com, Inc.

FIRST EDITION

ISBN: 9781521182369

Imprint: Independently published

Author's Biography

Garrett Kelley is a former National Security Agency analyst who worked during the Ronald Reagan presidency in the 1980's. He spent six years living first in southern Italy and then in northern Japan as a SIGINT analyst, then returned to private life in a variety of capacities, including typesetter, printer, home care coordinator, residential facility director, and home school cooperative leader. He currently teaches at a rural school in western Wisconsin where he lives with his wife, Ann, an emergency medical technician, and his two daughters.

Mr. Kelley spends his free time studying equity jurisprudence and how to attain equitable remedies in chancery (equity) court. He is part of a study group of several friends and fellow citizens who are committed to achieving fairness and justice in the practice of law. He plans to write another book very soon about how to access equity court (without being funneled into an administrative law court), a remedy guaranteed by Article III of the Constitution.

Preface

This story chronicles the events leading up to a Department of Homeland Security-ICE Homeland Security Investigations Raid of a Christian family's home, which included holding and interrogating two under-aged girls for over three hours about homeschooling, church activities, and family life. It also addresses the raid itself and the family's attempts to obtain justice for the invasion of privacy, which is an equitable matter. All attempts to date have been thwarted by the U.S. legal system. Therefore, this text is offered to the public, in the court of public opinion, in an effort to stop such miscarriages of police actions in the future.

All proceeds from the sale of this story will be deposited into a trust account for the college expenses of the three children (two of whom are now young adults) negatively impacted by the raid. I thank you for your interest in the story and your support of this effort to publish this account of the raid, which was facilitated by a fraudulent search warrant.

April 2009: Director of Homeland Security Janet Napolitano declares veterans, patriots, conservatives, and Christians potential threats

"See, he who is bound with wickedness,/And has conceived trouble and brought forth falsehood."

Psalms 7:14

It was April, 2009. My wife and I watched in disbelief as we viewed Janet Napolitano on a Sunday morning talk show vilifying veterans, patriots, conservatives, and Christians as potential "extremists." A few days later, she issued an unapologetic apology, stating that veterans had taken her statements the wrong way. The manner in which she characterized veterans, patriots, and Christians, those that have preserved this nation's freedoms for hundreds of years, as threats to America's existence was particularly disturbing. (For details, refer to John W. Whitehead's piece entitled "Operation Vigilant Eagle: Is This Really How We Honor Our Nation's Veterans?" on *The Rutherford Institute* website: https://www.rutherford.org/publications_resources/john_whiteheads_com mentary/operation_vigilant_eagle_is_this_really_how_we_honor_our_nati ons_veterans).

We stood there in front of our desktop computer after watching the Director of Homeland Security dishonor the sacrifices that veterans make for this country every day, including my wife's and my sacrifices, having served honorably in the United States Air Force. We felt so betrayed by our own government, that after feeling the initial stun, we were flooded with righteous indignation. It began to dawn upon us that the 2008 presidential election was a much greater shift in the pendulum on the political scale to the left; it was a subversive attempt to dismantle the values that Americans have held dear for the previous two centuries.

This was the "change" Barack Obama promised: a Nietzschean transvaluation of values -- that is, an effort to turn American values upside-down. Sean Hannity from Fox News and other online media journalists were right; we knew nothing about this man and his intentions for America. His master's thesis at Columbia had vanished without a trace. Precious little was known about his past, except that he hung out with domestic agitator Bill Ayers and was coached by Frank Marshall Davis, a true believer in communism. Disturbing rumors came out of his church in Chicago led my Reverend Jeremiah Wright. He professed to be a Christian, but his works, his off-hand comments, and his affiliation with Marxist ideology suggested that he carried on a façade to get elected. Like Hillary Clinton, he seemed to be a fan of *Rules for Radicals'* principles and axioms. He was elected in a tidal wave of goodwill, yet no one knew his intentions as he entered the White House in January, 2009.

After watching the Obama Administration start to systematically grow the Department of Homeland Security, indoctrinate kids with

Common Core curriculum in public school, infringe upon the constitutional rights of Christian-based business owners, attack tea party groups through the IRS, spy on U.S. citizens, and dismantle the United States military for the first two years of his presidency, my wife and I debated how we could resist his efforts using our First Amendment rights on the internet. We were aware that many Obama administration trolls were attacking commenters on conservative and Christian news websites as this excerpt from Natural News (as reported by Royce Chrystin from *YourNewsWire.com*) indicates:

> "In Canada, it has been publicly admitted that the government uses paid trolls to warp Internet discourse. The following comes from Natural News:
>
> *'Several years ago, Canada's CTV News aired a short segment about how its own government had been exposed for hiring secret agents to monitor social media and track online conversations, as well as the activities of certain dissenting individuals. This report, which in obvious whitewashing language referred to such activities as the government simply "weighing in and correcting" allegedly false information posted online, basically admitted that the Canadian government had assumed the role of secret online police.*
>
> *Needless to say, the U.S. government is also engaged in this kind of activity as well. For instance, the U.S. government has actually been caught manipulating discourse on Reddit and editing Wikipedia. When it comes to spying, there is nobody that is off limits for our spooks. It just came out recently that we even spied on three*

*French presidents, and they are supposed to be our
"friends."*

*And just like the UK, the U.S. government has a very
broad definition of "extremists." This has especially been
true since Barack Obama has been in the White House. If
you doubt this, please see my previous article entitled "72
Types Of Americans That Are Considered.'"*

In fact, several other journalists published online articles in 2011
about the troll/shill phenomenon. As a result, my wife and I
decided to fight back in the court of public opinion because we
thought that we could confront them in a way that would neutralize
their rhetoric. However, I was concerned about what would
happen to us as a result of this exercise of free speech; I told her,
"You know that the DHS is going to raid our house eventually,
right? Bullying is what communists do to their political
opponents." As she is a strong patriot and scrappy in general, she
did not care, so in 2011, she began to confront trolls on the
websites we frequented.

In the summer of 2012, I began to confront trolls and shills on
conservative websites such as *Newsmax.com, CNSNews.com, WND.com,*
and *Foxnews.com.* It did not take long before our computer was attacked:
in October 2012, our system was hacked and taken over by an outside
entity, presumably the DHS, NSA, or one of its surrogates. We began to

look for online articles that corroborated what we suspected was happening. We read several online articles about Edward Snowden and his whistleblowing activities about the NSA. Unfortunately, many of the articles written in 2011 have been taken down from the internet.

More recently, Scott Dadich of *Occupy.com* wrote a piece in August 2014 entitled "Edward Snowden, the Most Wanted Man in the World." In this piece, Snowden discusses the NSA's efforts to control dissent among U.S. citizens. As Snowden asserted, "the NSA was spying on the pornography-viewing habits of political radicals. The memo suggested that the agency could use these "personal vulnerabilities" to destroy the reputations of government critics who were not in fact accused of plotting terrorism (a key principle from Alynski's *Rules for Radicals*). The document then went on to list six people as future potential targets." Snowden's reaction: "'It's much like how the FBI tried to use Martin Luther King's infidelity to talk him into killing himself,' he says. 'We said those kinds of things were inappropriate back in the '60s. Why are we doing that now? Why are we getting involved in this again?'" While no one in my family had a "personal vulnerability," with the NSA's postmodern "morality," what would stop their operatives from planting child pornography on an American's computer if it does the job of silencing government critics?

With the information provided by Edward Snowden and my own experience as a former SIGINT analyst for the NSA, I was certain that it was a government hack, especially based on the timing of my online political activism as a conservative Christian with sympathy for the tea party movement. The computer began running really hard and loud, and I could not input on the keyboard; Control-Alt-Delete did nothing to stop whatever computer operation was running. All my attempts to take control of my computer system failed. I simply unplugged the machine and told my wife what happened. We began to feel dread at the inevitability of a raid of our house by the government apparatus in Washington, D.C.

The hacking continued through April 2014, about 15 times or so that I was aware. If it happened when I was home, I would immediately unplug the machine; however, there were times when our desktop computer was left on at night in sleep mode without our realizing it, so I was not as vigilant about it as I could have been.

In April 2014, I engaged a troll on *CNSNews.com* in a lengthy debate about the destructiveness of the Obama Administration's policies, including Obamacare, Cash for Clunkers, Common Core expansion, spying on U.S. citizens, etc. The troll debated me vigorously, but eventually simply started calling me names and issuing expletives left and right as trolls often do when their convoluted rhetoric fails. After a few moments of the troll's tirade, I simply wrote, "What? No stomach for reasoned debate?" He simply wrote that he likes Obama regardless of what I thought, and he stopped posting on the Discussion Topic for the night. I thought: "Yes! I finally was able to rhetorically trounce a troll off a conservative news website!"

A few months later, the dread I experienced about a potential DHS raid at my home, making my wife and kids vulnerable, finally manifested itself as reality. The government was doing a lot more than spying on my computer and online activities.

July 16, 2014: The Raid

"That which is crooked, can none make straight: and that which faileth, cannot be numbered."

Ecclesiastes 1:15

It was a sunny day at about 3:45pm CST, and the City of Home town, Wisconsin seemed as it always had been: peaceful and friendly. However, as I turned onto our dead-end street, my heart sank as I immediately noticed numerous Department of Homeland Security and Buffalo County Sheriff's Department vehicles parked across the street and in front of my driveway. I knew the day was going to come because of our political blogging activities, but the contrast between the intensity of the situation and the beautiful weather was striking.

I pulled into the driveway and opened my van door to be met by a sheriff's deputy, who I later learned was the site supervisor. He had an air of confidence about him, wearing a smile and striding purposefully.

"We have a search warrant to copy your laptop and all flash drives you have in your possession."

"And what if I refuse?" I replied.

"Then we will confiscate your laptop and all your flash drives anyway."

It was interesting at this point because I was holding my laptop case, which had my university laptop and a flash drive inside, but he did not attempt to take it from me.

"What is the charge?" I asked in a strangely calm tone of voice.

"We need to go inside; I'll explain there."

We went into the house, and the scene was chaotic. DHS agents were striding back and forth in constant movement, asking questions, consulting with each other, and making themselves at home. One of them, Anthony W. Castillo, appeared to be the agent in charge, because he sat on our loveseat in khaki shorts, a tee shirt, and tennis shoes, with a smirk on his face. He was about 5' 9", bald, and appeared to be roided up (he was excessively muscle-bound).

The deputy then told me that we were being investigated for file sharing of child pornography across international borders, which is an international crime. The agents then attempted to question me at this point, but I told them I did not intend to say anything.

I had an odd sense of peace about me, though, because I had wiped the hard drive clean just one week earlier on the computer from which my wife and I did our political blogging. I had been procrastinating on re-writing the hard drive for months, but I had an overwhelming urge to finally complete the task because I knew that the feds were accessing my system for roughly two years; it would suddenly start running loudly, inputting from the keyboard became impossible, and I could not shut it down. Most of the time, I either unplugged the computer or held the button in until it shut down. This occurred at least 15-20 times from about October, 2012 to April, 2014.

I went to the kitchen to lay my laptop on the table and to check on my wife, who was in tears. As an Emergency Medical Technician who worked with the supervising deputy on a regular basis, she was very embarrassed about the subject matter of the investigation and frantic about our two teenaged daughters, who were held against their will for over three hours while the agents waited for my wife to return from work at about 3:30pm. My wife told me that the two Buffalo County social workers had interrogated our daughters, asking questions about our church membership, homeschooling, and computer activities. They also asked whether or not we argued, engaged in abuse or neglect, etc.

At about 3:50pm, I gathered my wife and kids and went into our bedroom after I discovered that they had already been fully interrogated before I arrived.

"Are you ok?" I asked my wife and two daughters.

"They separated us and made us answer all kinds of questions," my youngest said. "They also tore up my bedroom and threw my rifle on the floor, then made me answer questions about what I use it for."

Both of my daughters were traumatized, and my wife was inconsolable.

I looked around in our bedroom. The agents had trashed it, dumping the contents of our nightstands and rifling through our dressers and closets.

"Why are you talking to these guys? They are going to use anything you say against us."

"I was brought up trusting officers, so I didn't think about it," my wife said, trembling. Her father was a retired police officer.

"Ok, what's done is done, but don't say anything else; I'll take it from here."

We came back out into the living room, where Castillo still sat there with a smirk on his face. His eyes were dancing with glee. He also made himself very comfortable on our loveseat, crossing his legs with his arm over the back of the couch.

I was convinced that he came from the Chicago office of the DHS; there was an SUV with Illinois license plates outside, and he reminded me of the guys from the south side because my father grew up there. He had related a number of stories of thuggery, and I witnessed it myself when visiting my grandmother in Midlothian when I was a kid. I was certain this guy had come from that side of town.

Castillo watched intently as my wife and I sat on the sofa.

I looked my wife directly into her eyes: "I did not do this," I insisted.

While my statement was poor reassurance after all that was happening, I could tell that there was some sense of relief in her eyes. My daughters sat down on the couch with us, and we huddled there together for a few minutes.

I saw the two Buffalo County social workers, Jessica Zitur and Danielle Schalinske, shoot a look at me then exit my home.

"It's past 4 o'clock; I have to attend to my online office hours," I told J.

I went into the kitchen to grab my laptop, which was not being examined. I sat down on the couch and logged in so that I could answer any of my online students' questions. After a minute or two, a DHS agent came into the room and told me to shut the laptop.

"You do not have permission to access the computer during this investigation," he said smugly. "Shut it down."

"These are my office hours; I am being paid to work during this timeframe, and you are preventing me from completing that work."

"You can complete your work after we are done here."

I shut the computer in frustration and returned it to the kitchen table. I noticed a DHS agent sitting at the kitchen table who was looking at his laptop opposite from me. His name was Kevin C. Wrona, from the Milwaukee office. He was not like the Chicago agents; he seemed like one of my University of Wisconsin roommates of twenty years earlier, sensible, reasonable, and with common sense.

"What evidence do you have?" I asked.

"Someone used your wifi connection to engage in internet file sharing of pornography with a minor in another country. Photos were exchanged on the internet, which is an international crime."

"Were the photos of boys, girls, or both?" I asked evenly.

He began to get agitated: "Why do you ask?"

"Just curious."

"The photos were of underaged girls." He began to relax again, and seemed a little deflated. Agents had already copied the hard drives of all our computers except my work laptop, and they apparently did not find anything the least bit interesting.

I watched as the agents huddled around our desktop computer in the dining room; they were spending an inordinate amount of time on it, which suggested that it was their target all along. This was the computer my wife and I had used for fighting off Obama Administration trolls on conservative and Christian alternative news websites. I stood there silently, thanking YHWH for urging me to wipe clean the hard drive just one week earlier. (Praise His name!)

Craig Beebe, another agent from the Chicago office, appeared to be getting frustrated. He sat in front of the computer, unable to find any evidence that he clearly expected to find. He, too, appeared to be roided up, about 5' 10" tall, even more muscle-bound than Castillo, and also bald. He looked at me.

"There is a computer file on your computer that shouldn't be here."

"What do you mean?" I asked, getting nervous.

"There is a program here that is commonly used by pornography users to block others from seeing what they are doing."

I looked over his shoulder. "I don't know what you're talking about. All the software that is loaded on the computer is standard Microsoft software and common programs such as Internet Explorer, Jing, and Visio. We downloaded a video game or two, but other than that, we did not load anything unusual on the system."

I began to relax again; they did not find anything. While I was puzzled about Beebe's claim that an illicit program was on the computer, I was sure that my family was not responsible for it. It is conceivable that someone had hacked into our wifi and used it to engage in illegal activities, but there were too many coincidences in this investigation: Janet Napolitano's declaration of war against Christians, conservatives, veterans, and preppers, the trolls, the articles about trolls, Snowden's revelations, and the behavior of the DHS agents, who acted more like kidnappers and thugs than professional law enforcement officers.

I stood silently for some time while they continued to run programs on the desktop computer. After several minutes, I returned to the living room and just waited with my wife and kids.

My wife quietly told me she overheard Castillo on the phone, mentioning Obama's name. She did not like his tone of voice, which she thought sounded like a minion reporting to his superior.

At about 4:40pm, my friend, D.S., drove up unexpectedly. I silently praised our father in heaven because he had studied law, the Constitution, and privacy issues, so his arrival was most welcome. I met him across the street and apprised him of what was happening in the house.

Without fear, he strode onto my driveway where he was met by several DHS agents, including Castillo.

"Who are you?" he demanded.

"My name is (D.S.). We are all private American Nationals, due civilian process. This is a private trust estate and you are trespassing on it."

Castillo became agitated, and with some silent cue, four agents and officers surrounded D.S. with chests puffed out and arms out from their sides in a threatening posture. There was only about 12" of D.S.'s personal bubble left.

D.S. is about 5' 7" tall, and about 130 pounds, so he could not look threatening if he tried. Also, as a man of God, he was peace-loving, honest, and sincere.

"Show me your identification," demanded Castillo.

"My name is (D.S.). I am a private American National."

Castillo became even more threatening: "Show me your i.d. now."

D.S. pulled out his Republic of Wisconsin identification, which I didn't think was going to be acceptable. However, he handed it to Castillo, who passed it to Mike Osmond. Osmond went into my garage and called someone (probably the Buffalo County dispatch) to check out the identification. Osmond came out and gestured that D.S. was ok, then all the officers and agents relaxed.

D.S. suddenly held out his hand with a beaming smile on his face: "Friends?!"

Castillo then smiled, shook his hand, relaxed, and slowly backed away, as did the other officers.

I stood there in amazement as my peace-loving friend had disarmed all of the officers and agents with an unofficial identification, a smile, and a handshake. However, he did not let the private status claim go.

"Again, we are private American Nationals, due civilian process."

The officers and agents continued to ignore him, seemingly carefree in their posture and attitude. They went back into the house, and D.S. and I followed.

D.S. and I sat on the sofa, and Castillo made himself at home on his favorite spot on the loveseat. He again adopted his smug, gleeful air as he smirked at us.

D.S. and I discussed our private status as we occasionally looked at Castillo. He continued to sit there, unmoved, for several minutes. He finally stated in a mocking tone, "That's just a conspiracy theory."

I maintained my private status, and he suddenly escalated very quickly: he arose from his seat and charged me and D.S. with his fists clenched and chest puffed out, taking puffing breaths through his pursed lips. I did not flinch but kept my gaze trained on his eyes as he quickly approached.

"It looks like that struck a nerve."

Castillo suddenly relaxed and backed up to his spot on the loveseat again. Another agent, Nathan Cravatta, entered the room, looking at Castillo.

"Do we need an intervention?"

Castillo answered with "no."

After a few moments, Castillo's smug demeanor returned: "You know we're just doing our job."

D.S. replied, "That's what the Nazi officers said at the Nuremberg trials."

Castillo didn't have a retort for that comment.

D.S. began to ask for the search warrant, which seemed to cause a commotion. Several DHS agents came into the room as Castillo pointed at it; it lay on an end table in the living room. D.S. inspected it.

"Where is the sworn affidavit that must accompany the search warrant?"

Castillo: "It's not here."

D.S.: "Where is it?"

Castillo: "We don't have to show it to you."

D.S.: "All search warrants must be supported by a sworn affidavit by the injured party. Where is it?"

Castillo: "Not here."

We examined the signatures on the search warrant, which were scribbled and I had to write the names in later:

Which things may contain evidence of a crime, specifically: Possession of Child Pornography 948.12(1m).

and requests that a search warrant be issued to search said property for the described evidence and authorizing the subsequent forensic examination of the electronic evidence.

NOW, THEREFORE, in the name of the State of Wisconsin you are commanded forthwith to search the property and return this warrant within 48 hours before the Circuit Court for *Buffalo County*, to be dealt with according to law.

Dated at Buffalo County, Wisconsin this 15th day of July, 2014.

BY THE COURT:

Circuit Court Judge Court Commissioner
Buffalo County *C. Michael Chambers*

ENDORSEMENT ON WARRANT

I hereby acknowledge receipt of this warrant on the *15* day of *July*, 2014, at *1:50 pm*

Affiant
Lee Engfer

D.S.: "Who is the affiant?

Castillo: silence.

D.S.: "This search warrant is invalid without a sworn affidavit."

Castillo: silence.

D.S.: "Who is the court commissioner who signed the affidavit?"

None of the agents or officers seemed to know who the affiant or the court commissioner was even though Buffalo County has only one judge and two court commissioners as I later discovered.

After that exchange, at about 5:10pm, D.S. told me that he had to leave to pick up a horse trailer, so we went onto the driveway with most of the agents and officers following. D.S. repeated his declaration of our status, then told me to get all the names and badges of every officer and agent that was present. I frantically began to write down the officers' and agents' names and badge numbers. When I was done, D.S. began asking more questions.

"Who's in charge here?"

I initially thought it was Castillo, but D.S. informed me that the County Sheriff must give permission for any investigation under his jurisdiction.

"Who's in charge here?" he repeated.

"Deputy Osmond," Castillo said.

"Garrett, go in the house and declare your status," D.S. instructed.

Osmond was just coming out of the house, standing on the linoleum by the front door. I stood about five feet from him and stated, "I am a private American National, due civilian process." My voice trailed off at the end of the sentence because of Deputy Osmond's reaction: he stood very still and did not say a word. An expression of worry came across his face. We stood there silently for a few moments, face to face, but he seemed frozen in place.

Osmond and I went into the kitchen where Craig Beebe was packing up my work laptop.

"Wait! I cooperated by giving you access to my laptop to copy; you said that if I cooperated, it would not be confiscated!"

"We're going to take it to another facility to have it forensically examined," Osmond said.

"And what if they plant evidence on it?!" I demanded, incredulous.

Again, Osmond's facial expression became worried, but Beebe continued to pack up the laptop, smug and gleeful.

D.S. had meanwhile left with my youngest daughter to participate in a rodeo event. Moments later, as the investigation was winding down, my son pulled into a spot across the street. He was visibly exhausted and dehydrated from operating a weed trimmer for five hours in the hot sun, and now an expression of concern washed over his face as he saw all the agents and officers.

Me: "J., are you feeling alright?"

J: "No. I'm very dehydrated."

DHS Agents Nathan Cravatta and Stephen Westover approached J. before he could enter the house and began questioning him in front of the garage.

Westover: "J., we have a few questions for you. Do you use the internet at home to watch pornography?"

J.'s face turned white and he collapsed into a lawn chair that was sitting just inside the garage. Neighbors were standing nearby, watching and listening. He doubled over, appearing to black out.

J. is the kindest, most loving, spiritually mature young man I have ever known, so I knew the allegations were false. He was also very sensitive to hostility towards him, so his reaction did not surprise me as these agents confronted him.

My wife emerged from the house and quickly examined J., with her EMT training and motherly concern taking charge.

"I'm taking J. to the hospital to get IV fluids; he is very dehydrated."

She whisked him away from the agents, helped him into the van, and left for Eau Claire. Meanwhile, I stood on my driveway alone and bewildered. What had just happened was clearly not a bona fide police investigation. I had the presence of mind, however, to get the Illinois license plates from the white SUV that was parked in front of the house, the same vehicle in which Craig Beebe and Anthony Castillo entered and left the area with my laptop in tow.

At about 5:30pm, I went inside to console R.A., my fifteen-year-old daughter, to hug her, and to reassure her the best I could after she and her younger sister had been held as what can most appropriately be termed as hostages for five hours.

The Aftermath

Blessed is the man that findeth wisdom,

and the man that getteth understanding.

Proverbs 3:13

When my brother-in-law and his wife who lived next door heard about the raid, they became fearful and shunned us, just as Alinsky's *Rules for Radicals* #13 predicts. Prior to the raid, we chatted with them almost daily; afterwards, we rarely saw them. My wife's father was somewhat sympathetic at first, but then avoided face-to-face contact with us for a few months. Rumors had spread through our home town that our household had committed some heinous crime, but no one seemed to know what the investigation concerned, which was somewhat of a relief; however, acquaintances and local business owners appeared to view us differently because they were no longer friendly or talkative.

Throughout this timeframe, however, D.S. and his wife showed us love and friendship. He offered to pay for my wife and I to enroll in a private citizenship class that addressed our status. As he explained it, public U.S. citizens are not parties to the Constitution because they are bondservants to their certificates of live birth, committed to paying off the national debt, which will never be paid. After experiencing what it feels like to be treated as "enemies, belligerents, and rebels," to borrow an expression from the Trading with the Enemy Act of 1917 (which was amended to include U.S. citizens in 1933 via the Emergency Banking Relief Act), my wife and I reluctantly agreed.

Over a three-day period, we learned about private trust law and how it can be used to regain the rights and privileges guaranteed by the Constitution. While the leader of the course did not fully understand private trust law as D.S. and I discovered after studying the topic ourselves, he demonstrated the history of the legislation in the 19th and early 20th centuries that in effect robbed Americans of their rights, freedom, and wealth, a crooked legacy that continues today. He also taught that, if we see our names in all capital letters, that is the title of a legal fiction, otherwise known as a sole corporation, creditor in commerce; it is not the name of a man or a woman as we have been bamboozled into believing. It is based on the Roman concept of *Capitus diminutio maxima*, defined by thelawdictionary.org as such: "In Roman law, a diminishing or abridgment of personality" and "[t]he highest or most comprehensive loss of status. This occurred when a man's condition was changed from one of freedom to one of bondage, when he became a slave. It swept away with it all rights of citizenship and all family rights." This fraud perpetrated on the American people occurred shortly after we were born when the certificate of live birth was filed. Because our mothers signed the certificate of live birth but our fathers did not (look up "signature" in *Black's Legal Dictionary*), we were all deemed bastards and therefore escheated property under the custodial care of the state, which explains why social workers can take children away from their parents (both parents and children are chattel, or state-owned property).

Shortly after taking the course, I drove to the Buffalo County Courthouse in Alma, Wisconsin on 8/11/14 to acquire the names of all the officers and agents that participated in the raid at my house and to view the sworn affidavit that supposedly contained evidence against my household. My wife and my son accompanied me as I walked up to the Clerk of Court's office with the search warrant in my hand at about noon. I found Clerk of Court Roselle Schlosser there.

"Hi. I had a search warrant served at my home on 7/16/14, and I would like to know who signed it." I pointed to the scribbles on the search warrant.

"That was C. Michael Chambers, a court commissioner here."

"How about the affiant?"

"I don't know who signed that."

"How can I find out? Is there someone who can tell me?"

"You should try the Sheriff's Department; Mike Schmidtknecht should be in today."

"Ok, I'll try that. I would also like to see the affidavit that supported the search warrant."

Ms. Schlosser suddenly became officious, picked up a 9" by 12" sealed envelope that was lying in a tray within three feet of the window. She began waving it emphatically under my nose.

"The judge has sealed the affidavit so you are not permitted to look at it."

I became even more skeptical about the validity of the affidavit.

"Why not?"

"Judge Duvall will be here for a couple of hours; you can write a request to view it, and I'll put it on his desk."

"Ok, do you have a piece of paper?"

She gave me a notepad, upon which I wrote a note to the judge, respectfully requesting to view the affidavit that supported the search warrant. I thanked her, then my wife, J., and I walked down the hall to the sheriff's department.

We were buzzed in after waiting for a few minutes. We sat on some chairs outside a security door while the sheriff was notified of our arrival. He came into the waiting room and asked us what we wanted.

"Can you tell me who signed this search warrant as affiant?"

The sheriff's demeanor became frazzled and a little nervous. "That was Lee Engfer; he is a Buffalo County Sheriff's Deputy."

"I would also like to know the names of everyone who was in my house that day."

This question seemed to make him very nervous. He started to walk one direction, then went another. "I'll have to check in my office; I'll be right back."

We waited patiently for a few minutes until he returned. He gave us the names of his deputies and the Buffalo County Social Workers. "I don't know the names of the DHS Agents."

"That's ok; I already have their names and badge numbers."

He hesitated a moment and looked genuinely apologetic. "I apologize for what you went through."

He held out his hand, so I took it calmly and respectfully, but I only said, "Thanks."

D.S. told me later that the sheriff is a fellow believer, and he certainly appeared to be genuinely apologetic.

We left the sheriff's department and went out to lunch, hoping that the judge would get my note so that we could view the affidavit.

We returned a couple of hours later.

"Has the judge been in yet?"

Roselle: "He was here for a few minutes, but he left right away; I don't think he saw the note on his desk." She instructed the deputy clerk, Ashley Henthorn, to check. Ashley returned with the note in her hand.

Ashley: "It appears that he didn't get it."

Roselle: "You can request a hearing before the judge to view the affidavit."

After my private citizenship class, I did not intend to submit myself to a statutory court where I was viewed as an enemy, belligerent, and rebel. To be treated as a human being, I needed to access chancery court, otherwise known as equity jurisdiction, which is supposedly accessible in Wisconsin.

I became a bit testy: "Never mind; I have all the information I need."

To Ashley: "Just write a note stating that you refused to allow me to view the affidavit."

Ashley: "I am not refusing to allow you to view the affidavit; you can request a hearing."

"Well, put it any way you like. How about 'Garrett Kelley was not permitted to view the affidavit in connection with the search warrant served on his home on 7/16/14?'"

She agreed, so I wrote it out and then she signed it, but it looked like she merely printed her name.

"Do you mind signing the document?"

Ashley: "I did."

"It looks like you printed your name."

"Oh, that's the way I sign my name."

"Ok, fair enough. Thanks."

I left with the signed document and returned home, scanned it into my computer, and discussed the outcome with D.S. He was disgusted when he heard how Roselle waved the affidavit just beyond my reach. D.S. asked me to travel with him to Madison, Wisconsin to file a bill in equity in the District Court of Western Wisconsin and to retrieve his original certificate of live birth, which was signed by his mother. This appeared to be an engaging bit of investigative reporting, so I agreed.

Security screened us, requesting the purpose of our visit. The security officers became a little agitated when D.S. told them that he was filing a bill in equity. After some confused gawking, they directed us to the elevator.

D.S. approached the public desk for filing cases and suits (although the process for filing an equity suit is highly secretive). A young man who D.S. later called a desk troll came to meet him.

D.S.: "I have a bill in equity that I would like to file."

Troll: "Do you mean a lawsuit?"

D.S.: "No, it is a suit in equity, in chancery court."

Troll: "I don't know what you're talking about."

D.S.: "The Constitution of the United States guarantees an equitable remedy for private citizens."

The troll sat down at his desk without saying a word, and as though there were some unspoken cue, an older woman came from behind a partition to wait on D.S. Her name was Joanne Freidl. She helped D.S. with assigning a chancery court number that had a capital "C" in front of the number in contrast to civil statutory cases, which started with "CV." Another distinction is that statutory cases will always list the parties' names in all capital letters, as corporations, while equity cases will have the names properly spelled in upper and lower case letters. It is referred to as "in personam" jurisdiction, or as I like to say, as human beings.

However, if one's paperwork does not show "trust" and one's filing does not reserve common law and equitable rights, the federal court is very adept at snatching the $400 filing fee and funneling the case back into statutory court. The magistrate judge, Peter Oppeneer, is the stumbling block to getting a case into equity court because he funnels equity suits into statutory civil cases unless they abide by some secret, undisclosed process. During a phone call, Ms. Freidl hinted that most people mail bills in equity, but she frankly told D.S. that she could not give any legal advice in an exasperated tone.

After we finished at the federal court building, we proceeded to our next stop. When we arrived at the Department of Human Services in the Vital Records Department, a woman in her late 20's or early 30's came to the window. I sat down on a chair directly across from the window as D.S. engaged her.

"I would like to see the wet-ink original certificate of live birth that my mother signed when I was born."

The clerk became very agitated. "I can't let you see it."

"Why not?"

"It's not here."

"Isn't this the Office of Vital Statistics?"

"Yes, but we only issue birth certificates.

"I'm not interested in my birth certificate; I can get that in my home county. I would like to see the original certificate of live birth."

She became more agitated. "I'll get someone to talk to you."

She was gone for about ten minutes, and peace-loving D.S. stood there patiently and shot a smile at me. I smirked in reply.

A woman in her 50's and a younger man in his early 30's came to the window at the same time. D.S. repeated his request.

Woman, nervously: "We don't have it here."

D.S.: "Isn't this office the place where all vital records are kept?"

Woman: "Yes, but we only have a copy of it."

D.S.: "Where is the original?"

Woman: "We have it in storage."

D.S.: "Please bring it here so I can see it."

Woman: "It is an original copy."

D.S.: "What does that mean? I would like to see the "wet ink" original certificate of live birth."

Woman, frazzled: "We don't have the original."

Man interjects: "I can give you contact information of the unit supervisor if you like; she should be able to give you more information. She is not available today, though, so you'll have to call."

D.S. agreed after some hesitation. He expressed his disappointment with the result to me, but he had made video/audio recordings of the interchanges with a hidden camera while we visited the district court and Department of Human Services employees; he could demonstrate the duplicitous nature of the bureaucrats: there was a secret process for filing bills in equity, and the Department of Human Services employees were obviously very anxious about concealing his certificate of live birth, which is the original offending, fraudulent document that classified him as a bondservant.

After we returned home, I attempted to file a bill in equity in federal court against the Department of Homeland Security and Buffalo County, but the magistrate kicked it out of equity and entered it in statutory court. After two tries, I gave up that effort and waited for D.S. to discover the appropriate avenue for a bill in equity, a highly secretive process that does not appear to be published anywhere. Meanwhile, I reduced my spoken declaration of trust with the agents and officers to writing in the form of a trust, then mailed copies to Castillo, Engfer, and Osmond, the key players in the fraudulent raid on my home. I challenged them to disclaim or disavow my testimony about all that occurred during the investigation, and of course they did not because they have been conditioned by the statutory court system to remain silent at all costs. However, in trust law, if one does not disclaim or disavow a trust, then by one's silent acknowledgment, one becomes a trustee be default, just as a biological father is a trustee of the state's when he does not sign the certificate of live birth as natural father and beneficiary of his wife's gift (the baby). That is the mechanism by which the state can enforce child support but take away visitation rights simultaneously: as a trustee, the biological father has no rights if the statutory court rules against him regarding visitation rights.

While I waited for D.S. to discover the appropriate process, I filed a complaint with the DHS Office of Civil Rights and Civil Liberties in October of 2014. After a few months, the office responded in what appears to be a form letter (there is no signature) as such:

Clearly, the DHS complaint process wastes victim

> The U.S. Department of Homeland Security's (DHS) Office for Civil Rights and Civil Liberties (CRCL) received information from you on October 8, 2014. Thank you for bringing your concerns to our attention.
>
> After carefully reviewing the information you provided, CRCL has recorded the issues you have raised in our database so that we can track those issues in order to identify patterns of violations of civil rights, civil liberties, and profiling on the basis of race, ethnicity, or religion by employees and officials of the Department of Homeland Security. CRCL will take no further action on your information at this time. For more information about CRCL's roles and responsibilities, please visit our website at http://www.dhs.gov/crcl.
>
> Please be advised that CRCL does not provide individuals with legal or procedural rights or remedies. Accordingly, CRCL is not able to obtain any legal remedies or damages on your behalf. Instead, we use information in correspondence like yours to find and address problems in DHS policy and its implementation. If you believe your rights have been violated, you may wish to consult an attorney. There may be time limitations that govern how quickly you need to act to protect your interests.
>
> Please note that Federal law forbids retaliation or reprisal by any Federal employee against a person who makes a complaint or discloses information to CRCL. 42 U.S.C. § 2000ee-1(e). If you believe that you or someone else is a victim of such a reprisal, please contact us immediately.
>
> Thank you again for contacting the Office for Civil Rights and Civil Liberties. Inquiries like yours help DHS meet its obligation to protect civil rights and civil liberties.
>
> Sincerely,
>
> Office for Civil Rights and Civil Liberties
> U.S. Department of Homeland Security

s' time, so I gave up getting any kind of remedy that route. My wife and I waited patiently for D.S. to discover another avenue by which we could submit our bill in equity.

In February of 2015, D.S. found an interesting clause in a Wisconsin statute that seemed to permit complainants (not plaintiffs) in equity to file a bill in state circuit court: "**990.07 Evidence.** The Wisconsin statutes as prepared under s. 35.18 shall be prima facie evidence in all courts and proceedings as provided by s. 889.01; *but they shall not preclude reference to, nor control, in case of any discrepancy, any original act of the legislature*; and the certified volumes of the Laws of Wisconsin provided for by s. 35.15 shall also and in the same degree be prima facie evidence in all courts and proceedings" (https://docs.legis.wisconsin.gov/statutes/statutes/990). Because Chancery Court was established in 1849 in an original act of the legislature and a discrepancy existed (statutory court cannot take jurisdiction over matters of private trusts), this appeared to be a veiled doorway into equity. I began to study the Wisconsin statutes as well and discovered the front door, as it were, dealing with the right to privacy:

995.50   Right of privacy.
(1)   The right of privacy is recognized in this state. One whose privacy is unreasonably invaded is entitled to the following relief:
(a) **Equitable relief** to prevent and restrain such invasion, excluding prior restraint against constitutionally protected communication privately and through the public media;
(b) Compensatory damages based either on plaintiff's loss or defendant's unjust enrichment; and
(c) A reasonable amount for attorney fees.

(2) In this section, "invasion of privacy" means any of the following:
(a) Intrusion upon the privacy of another of a nature highly offensive to a reasonable person, in a place that a reasonable person would consider private or in a manner which is actionable for trespass.
(Excerpt from

https://docs.legis.wisconsin.gov/statutes/statutes/995/50)

When the term "equitable relief" appears in a statute, it indicates a pathway to an equitable remedy, otherwise known as the appropriate circumstance under which one may file a bill in equity. D.S. and I became excited about our finds; we began to prepare our suits in equity for filing in the state's circuit courts.

We filed our suits in February of 2015 in Buffalo County Circuit Court in Alma, Wisconsin. We chose to use court classification code 30703 (unclassified) because there were no codes for bills in equity. We expected that the sheriff would serve the suits in accordance with the process laid out in Gibson's *Suits in Chancery*, but service never took place. Eventually, after a few months, both cases were dismissed for lack of service. However, since the fee was only $164.50, the lesson learned was not quite as painful as it was in the U.S. District Court of Western Wisconsin.

On a lark, D.S. and I drove down to Alma again in March 2015 to do some research on oaths of office. I agreed because his jaunts were both educational and entertaining, and I wanted to ask a few questions of my own. When we arrived, D.S. requested the oaths of office of Judge James Duvall and Sheriff Mike Schmidtknecht, which turned up some surprises. The oaths of office of the judge and court commissioners had the following nullification clause: "but have not yet entered upon the duties thereof":

STATE OF WISCONSIN, CIRCUIT COURT, _____ BUFFALO _____ COUNTY

For Official Use
CIRCUIT COURT
FILED
JUL 31 2012
ROSELLE M. SCHLOSSER
CLERK OF COURT

Oath of Office for
Court Commissioners

I, who have been appointed to the office of

☐ circuit court commissioner
☒ supplemental court commissioner

for this county, but have not yet entered upon the duties thereof, do solemnly swear that I will support the Constitution of the United States and the Constitution of the State of Wisconsin, and will faithfully discharge the duties of this office to the best of my ability. So help me God.

_____
Signature
C. Michael Chambers
Name Printed or Typed
July 30, 2012
Date

Apparently, at the time of signing the oath, the judge and court commissioners were not yet entering upon their constitutional oaths. In addition, the oath indicated that they merely "support" the Constitution; they do not "uphold, protect, and defend" it as enlistees in the military promise. D.S. said that he believes that judges in Wisconsin are merely attorneys dressed in black robes because of the bogus oath of office.

I did my own research: it turns out that the Court Commissioner who signed the search warrant used by DHS-ICE and Buffalo County Sheriff's Department, according to the deputy clerk of court Ashley Henthorn, was named C. Michael Chambers, an attorney from Fountain City, Wisconsin. Deputy Henthorn gave me a copy of Mr. Chambers' last commission, which expired in 2012. Interestingly, he signed the search warrant on July 15, 2014:

STATE OF WISCONSIN, CIRCUIT COURT, _____ **BUFFALO** _____ COUNTY | For Official Use

IN THE MATTER OF THE
APPOINTMENT/AUTHORIZATION OF:

C. Michael Chambers
_____ as Circuit Court Commissioner _____

**Order
Appointing/Authorizing
Circuit Court
Commissioner**

State Bar No.: _1016690_

IT IS ORDERED:

1. The above-named person is:
   ☐ appointed a circuit court commissioner for the above-named county under SCR 75.02(1). This person must be an attorney with at least 3 years of legal experience.
   ☒ authorized under SCR 75.02(3), as a supplemental court commissioner for the above-named county, to perform specific duties as set forth below on a temporary or occasional basis. This person must:
      • be an attorney, with at least 3 years of legal experience, and
      • have been appointed a supplemental court commissioner under §757.675(1) Wis. Stats.
   ☐ appointed to supervise the office of family court commissioner for the county under §757.68 (2m) (a) 1, or (b) Wis. Stats.

2. This appointment/authorization shall:
   ☒ be from (date) _October 1, 2008_ to (date) _July 31, 2012_ ; or
   ☐ commence on (date) _____ and be subject to annual recertification.

3. The Honorable _James J. Duvall_
   is/are appointed supervising judge(s) for the circuit court commissioner and shall:
      • communicate responsibilities and performance objectives, and
      • conduct annual written evaluations, and
      • submit annual written recertification recommendations.

Me: "Do you know C. Michael Chambers?"

Deputy Henthorn: "No, I don't."

Me: "Could you give me a copy of his oath of office and his last commission?"

Deputy Henthorn: "Yes, but there will be a charge per copy."

Me: "That's fine."

She left for a few minutes into a room just off the clerk's office. She returned with a copy of his oath of office and the commission. I noticed immediately that it expired in 2012.

Me: "Are you sure that is the last commission for C. Michael Chambers?

Deputy Henthorn: "Yes. There are no more recent copies in the file."

Me: "Ok, very interesting. Thank you for your assistance."

D.S. and I remained in the hallway, stunned by what we discovered. We spoke in hushed tones about the revelation I discovered that an attorney operating out of Cochrane, Wisconsin signed the search warrant. Could it be that the DHS-ICE investigation was so sloppy and crooked that the agents sought out a search warrant from an attorney instead of a bona fide court commissioner? Just then, the D.A., Thomas

Clark, approached us down the hallway. I later discovered that he was the one who requested that the affidavit to the search warrant be sealed.

D.S.: "Do you know C. Michael Chambers?

He stood there for a moment searching his memory. "I haven't seen him around for a couple years."

D.S.: "So he doesn't work for the county?

D.A. Clark: "No."

Hmmm.

D.S.: "Ok, thank you," he said with a huge grin.

D.S. and I go to the County Clerk's office downstairs. We found the assistant because the County Clerk was gone for the day.

D.S.: Do you know C. Michael Chambers?

Assistant clerk: "No, I don't."

D.S.: "We're trying to find out if C. Michael Chambers is a county employee. Can you help us?"

Assistant clerk: "I will try; I'm filling in today because the County Clerk is gone for the day."

D.S.: "Can you check personnel files to see if C. Michael Chambers is employed with Buffalo County?"

Assistant clerk: "I'll check for you. It will be a few minutes because I don't usually do this job."

D.S., with his disarming smile: "That's fine, we're patient."

She looked through some personnel files for a few minutes, then stepped into the hallway where we waited.

Assistant clerk: "No, I don't have any record of employment for C. Michael Chambers."

D.S.: "Thank you very much!"

We left the courthouse with this revelation in mind, not sure about our next steps.

Postscript

In March, 2015, D.S. and I met with the Buffalo County Sheriff about the oaths of office of the public officers of Buffalo County, alleging that the oaths were not constitutional. The sheriff showed us his oath of office, which was indeed constitutional in wording and content, but the judge's and court commissioners' were not. At our request, he sent an email to J.B. Van Hollen, the Wisconsin State Attorney General requesting clarification on why sheriff's deputies have a constitutional oath of office but not judges and court commissioners. His office soon after responded by merely stating that the oaths of office were valid.

In September, 2015, I spoke with Dale Goss, the operations manager of NTEC, our internet service provider because I was setting up new service and had concerns about the connection. During the conversation, I told him of my concerns about security of my system and hacking, and I related what happened with the DHS-ICE. I asked him if NTEC informed the DHS of the alleged internet child pornography file sharing on my internet connection at my former address, and he said, "No. We don't share internet activities of our customers with any outside agencies or companies." I replied that DHS agents claimed that NTEC reported the internet file sharing of child pornography. He became very nervous on the phone and repeated that DHS's claim was not true.

In 2016, I spoke with an attorney, Mr. Fox from the Milwaukee area about the viability of filing a lawsuit against the DHS. He delivered the bad news that, if I couldn't demonstrate any clear financial damage as a result of the raid, there was no case. I related how my daughters were held against their will for 3 hours and interrogated by Buffalo County Social Workers Danielle Schalinske and Jessica Zitur, as well as DHS agents, but he informed me that emotional or psychological distress was very difficult to prove without a physical injury of some sort. I mentioned my son's trip to the emergency room, but Mr. Fox said that attorneys for the DHS would simply say that it was from dehydration, not from public humiliation and/or slander. While I did not gather useful information, I was grateful for an attorney who finally took the time to explain my legal options or lack thereof.

In May of 2016, I sent Mr. Goss a letter demanding formal discovery of his comments on the phone, written, signed, and sworn before a notary public, for an equity suit I filed in the Court of Chancery of the State of Delaware. He lawyered up and refused to cooperate. My suit was dismissed in early June.

While this story has not fully concluded, justice in the form of equity, guaranteed by Article III of the Constitution for the United States of America, appears out of reach for the common person. The only "justice" attainable, therefore, is in the court of public opinion. I have shared this story out of righteous indignation, not just for my wife, my children, and I, but also for all other conservatives, Christians, veterans, and patriots who have experienced similar intrusions. It is my hope and prayer that our country's great tradition of equity and equal treatment under the law have been saved from utter destruction because of Trump's election, but clearly, the fight has just begun.

.

Made in United States
Troutdale, OR
07/27/2024